This Exit

With Millennialism & New Poems

Joshua C. Robinson

Joshua C. Robinson

This Way To Exit, Much Madness, Millennialism & New Poems

DEDICATION

To my parents, my family, my teachers, and my friends.
Without all of you, I would be very lonely indeed.

To Krew and Zephaniah, the future is yours, take it!

ACKNOWLEDGMENTS

This book would not have been possible without the patience of some very exceptional people. Scott Ray Merchant, whose guidance and edits played a key role in this current version of "This Way To Exit". My ex, who I won't name out of courtesy. My parents, whose encouragement pushed me onward. My sisters, who amaze and astound me daily. My teachers, who dealt with my endless experimentation with the written word, and late assignments. And my friends, who listen even when I'm not listening to myself.

Joshua C. Robinson

This Way To Exit

(Darkness, footsteps, the metallic sound of a light cord being pulled, and the stage is bathed in a 60 watt glow. A man in a black suit, black tie, white shirt is revealed.)

(AN: There is a presence of a guardian angel throughout the entire proceedings that can be incorporated to assist or impede Josiah with visual representation of his words, handing him or the audience items or physically interacting with him. This angel is unseen to Josiah, and can be played by either gender. The inclusion of this angel is a matter for the director to decide)

JOSIAH HESSE

(Primal, Deep, Echoing)
FUUUUUUUUUUUUUUUUUUUUUUUUUUUUUUU—CK,
YEEEEESSSSS!

Thought I'd get that out of the way.

You know that climactic point in the play when everything has gone wrong or right, and the hero is gouging out his eyes, the prince has found his true love.
I just thought it best, to...get the end out of the way, before we begin. My name's Josiah by the way. Josiah Hesse. I've been told I'm here to entertain you.

I hope I do, otherwise I might as well
masturbate on-stage.

My we're looking good tonight, all of you, me
included. What a fantastic looking crowd, and
performer. Intelligent too. I can tell from
the way your eyes look, that you are all very,
deeply, tragically intelligent.

I can't see your eyes. The lights, you know. I
wanted to make you feel good, at ease. My
mother told me that compliments do that. A
breaking of the ice, as it were. Do you like
my eyes? Can you see them?

If you could they'd tell stories, we could
stare at each other the whole night long, like
lovers entangled in an oh so small bed. We'd
know each other. Yes all of you and me, we'd
know each other, Biblical... and spiritually,
but our eyes would gaze deep in, and you would
know me, I would know you, a surfeit of words
pulsing between our eye contact. Our
mysteries absolved and spread like butter
against each-others minds.

But you can't see my eyes, and I can't see
yours. I suppose that's why I'm here. On this
stage. I can't very well go to bed with all
of you at once. I think I might like to
though; given societal norms that might be a
bit...
much. Later perhaps. Later. A day later.

We measure time so strangely, a day, the earth
rotates, a year, the earth swings all the way
around the sun. However old you are that's

how many times the world has spun around the
sun. It's all relative. Everything. Lord
knows how fast our galaxy is rocketing through
space. Think about that. Each year, our
galaxy, rushing through an empty black web.
So fast it can't be measured because there is
nothing to measure it by. There's no zero
galaxy, there isn't a galaxy that just sits
there, in one spot. And this big bang thing.
Wormholes, drains in the universe that lead to
another part of the universe. Black holes,
white holes, all this expansion and
contraction. All this ebb and flow.
Imagine yourself lifting off the ground,
rushing out past poor demoted Pluto. you're
rushing faster now, past Sirius B, and out the
Milky Way the Horsehead Nebula behind you all
that swirling red, orange, and white, and your
still going at it, still rocketing forward,
still flying out, out of the supercluster of
our known galaxies, and you just
keep rocketing out, all these tiny Christmas
lights behind you. There's millions and
millions of galaxies behind you, and they all
look so damn small now, just a pinprick, and
more pin pricks rush by all of the collecting
at this tiny point, and you see it the limits
of this universe, just a field of black, the
space where even light can't reach, this
curtain, the final bow, and you break through.
You've done it limit beyond limit, your
ripping through that black curtain, you want
this you want the beyond, and you push out.
Out. OUT.

(Josiah should express
vulnerability
and fear at this moment.)
Here you are. In a field of white, you're so
weak you can't rub your eyes, and you're
spanked, you breathe you cry, held by your
feet, your arches so
thick against those blue gloves, and all you
want is to feed, and she smiles back at you.
Your mother just smiles, and gives you milk.

That's it. The edge of never. The beginning of
everything. Maybe that's what happens when
everything ends, eh? Reboot, Reset, Retry.
It'd be a blessing wouldn't? If God just drops
us back in.

We've been in the dugout so long. So long.
We've forgotten how to play.

We played when we were children, you and I.
We all got along and played tag and girls and
cooties, but that one girl, she didn't have
cooties. Her hair was so gold and your palms
were so sweaty. Everyone brings girls flowers
right? So you pick some daisies, you stroll up
to her, ready to kiss her like Cary Grant,
you're James Bond, You're Luke Skywalker,
You're freakin' Bruce Wayne, and you picked
the biggest brightest daisies, you stroll up
like you won the lottery and half of it was
for her. Her name was Casey, she was gold.
You hold out those daisies, ready to take her
away on that black stallion you don't have,
and ride to that cabin in the soft white snow,
you're ready to lift her to the heavens and
soar because you have wings dammit, right

here, this moment, you have wings. She knocks
the flowers to the ground and runs away
screaming, "boys have cooties."
You fall to the ground and cry, cry because
she left you, cry because the movies lied, and
you cry because you'll know this moment again
and every time, you'll remember the edge of
never, that big black curtain.

You want a knife to cut through it, every time
you want a knife, and all you ever have is a
spoon. Would you like some ice cream?

I would love some.
                    (Goes to table, there is
                    ice cream, begins eating
                    it.)

Ice cream. It's so simple, so pleasurable. I
feel like there has to be something profound
about it. The secret to the universe
contained in it. Cold. Frozen. Cream.
There's just something magical about it. Maybe
it's the cure, for... for everything. Like
honey. Imagine honey, endless amounts of
honey, distilled, purified, concentrated, put
into pills. Curing cancer, AIDS, war, all
disease. Hell, honey curing death. I mean
just imagine it. This viscous natural syrup,
curing everything. The cure... for
everything. I told this to a doctor once.
Honey it's the cure for everything. "Are you
writing this down?" It will cure AIDS, and
cancer. Hope is in honey. He just smiled and
nodded. Held up an inkblot. "What does this
look like?" What do you mean what does it look
like? It looks like a fucking inkblot. Sorry,

was that too much. We don't know each-other
well enough. That doctor. Honey.
                    *(Josiah is emotionally
collapsing)*
But the honey-bees are dying. Are they really
dying? I mean, come on! All the honey-bees,
in the world, dying? It's too much. We
wouldn't survive. Yet, here we are. I hope
you didn't want any ice cream. Or Daisies.
                    (Snapping back to confidence.)
My only wife Casey. I married her. I live in
Southern California, I have an estate, and a
vineyard. The wine from those grapes, so good
the government has yet to make it a felony,
but they will, that good. Wine this good,
it's like honey, it cures things.

It's a good wine to make love on.
Prescription: Two glasses, Cabernet Sauvignon,
fermented from those grapes you know so well,
on your soil, outside your windows. Two people
hopelessly in love. Two sets of under things
discarded. Two hours of earth-shaking love.
Two hearts, beating, du-thub, du-thub. Two
hours exhausted, sharing sweat, all that
breath pouring between you. Two days with
nothing but time, and wine, and sex. That will
cure everything. Who needs dying when you
have that?

Doctor's orders, two in bed, stay till
recovered, repeat as needed. Unlimited
refills. If only you could see my eyes.
They'd arrest you, you wouldn't be able to
move. And we can't make love. We're trying
though, me up here, you out there, lord knows
we're trying.

If I ever saw it. Humans should have wings.
We should have them, for purely practical
reasons, not to mention the delight, but you
know, to get around. No more of this car
nonsense. Going to the grocery store to get a
quart of milk. Have wings, will fly. No more
of this falling to your death nonsense.
Always taking the most direct line to every
destination. And everyone has always wanted
to fly, even if you're afraid of heights, and
with wings there would be no reason to be
afraid, even then, afraid of heights, just a
little bit of hovering. We've all wanted to
fly. Humans should have wings.

> *(pause with utmost*
> *sincerity)*

Humans do have wings.

> *(pause)*

Maybe this is your last time around. Shit…

Anyway… A dog followed me around the other
day, for the afternoon, I bent down and pet
the poor thing, all black, white feet like
socks, little puppy socks. I just pet it, for
maybe twenty seconds. And it followed me
around for the rest of the day. What was
going through that dog's head? I'll never
know. I'll never know and that kinda freaks
me out. This dog, I show it the bare minimum
of love, it's impossible not to, the black
little thing coming up and licking my hand,
putting its little paw socks on me. I love it
for an instant and it's hooked. It doesn't
know that I might have betrayed countless
loves before, sent entire fleets of lovers to
the grave. I could be a sociopath for all

this dog knows, just reacting in what my
deranged mind believes to be a compassionate
series of appropriate actions. I might even
be Joseph Stalin, and this puppy trusts me,
completely, trusts me like family, like twin
brothers. Like this dog knows me. Like it
knows me better than I know myself. Like this
dog actually *sees* my fucking wings.
(pause)

I'm not. Not a sociopath, at least... I don't
think so. They say that intelligence
correlates with sociopathic tendencies. The
more computations you're able to do in your
head, the more brilliant poems you produce,
the more films that define what it means to
look, to gaze into all that human condition,
the more you are capable of, the more measured
your reaction to humanity. If you meet any
fiercely intelligent people everything must be
calculated, even their friendships. But what
isn't calculated is death.

(pause)

I should tell you about myself.
You're not gonna like it.
You won't believe me.
I'm dead.
my wings.
Can you see them?
Maybe not.
I hope you can see them.
Someday.
They're beautiful. I didn't make them, but
they're so damn beautiful you forget what it
is to breathe, so beautiful

I had wings then, oh did I ever have wings. I
still have wings. Did I mention that, me being
dead. Forgive my abstractions. I'm still
getting used to using language again.
Bonjour.
Guten-Tag.
Hola.
Hello.
I'm waiting. For the next thing.
Being dead isn't so boring you know. Gives you
perspective. Not like, a better view on
things. It actually gives you perspective.
Imagine drawing stick figures your whole life,
never knowing anything more, and then a man
comes up
to you with HD video equipment, editing
software, 3D rendering software, and movie
studio. And as he's walking away he drops all
the hallucinogens in the world, and says,
"this is just the first part. There's people
who have reached Nirvana and they have smiles
so big you'd think they bought them from a
store. There are mountains that go as high as
spaceships. Wonders out here man, wonders!"

That's like life and death. There are stick
figures, and there's *all that*.

Death renders you more capable than life. Play
any instrument, perform Hamlet as a man or a
woman or anything in between. I can do all of
it. So that's what I'm doing…

No pain.
Or sadness.

Or suffering.
We're all fit Buddhas.
Mondays don't exist.
Days don't exist, but Mondays? They especially
don't exist.
Time is interesting. All of it exists at
once, and it has a heartbeat. That big black
curtain pulses like your heart. The Universe
breathes time in and out like air.

On this stage, I can't really tell. Am I back
from Heaven? Or am I on my way? What happens
next? I thought I knew, I didn't. I don't
think I do.

Time existing as it does, Vonnegut style, all
at once.
On this stage, I think I'm alive. I feel, and
I'm worried about what you might think of me.
And I'm worried that

what I'm saying might not get to you. I want
to make you cry, and I want to make you laugh.
I want you to sweat, and drip for me. I want
to make love to all of you.

We could try, you know?

> *(adjusts tie, coughs,
> asking)*

I could use that new technique with auras and
energy, and a few kinky toys.

We could make love from vast distances. Maybe
we're making love right now. Time being what
it is.

"The best ever," I said.
So you said too.
But we both know that we had better.

We were just being polite. It was decent
though. Sex is an insane act, if you really
think about it. Trusting someone enough to be
inside you, you inside them. People the world
over are busy murdering each other, and you
let someone get that close to you, entwined
with you. It's madness.
                    (Josiah deflates)
Madness, I was always more afraid of that than
death. I don't know what comes next. After
insanity, the long struggle. I don't know
what's after death. I'm dead and I don't know,
because I'm also alive. I'm still trying to
figure it out. I remember my life. I know
what comes after birth.
                    (Back to confidence)
I'm gonna empty my pockets now.

                         *(proceeds to do so, and
                         with each item a story.)*
A gum wrapper.
When I was young there was this special kind
of juicy gum, with zebras on the wrapper, and
it was covered in stripes.
Everyone had this kind of gum. I would jump
up and down at the grocery store, begging my
father to buy it. We were always in the
checkout line, this seems to be the best
place to get parents to buy things for you.
I'm jumping up and down, "Please dad, please,
I'll be good forever. I'll vacuum my room.
I'll take the dog out for two walks a day.

I promise. I'll be the best. I'll be so good.
I won't ask for anything for Christmas, please
dad please!" My father would always put on a
big show about whether or not to get the gum.
"Hmmm, I dunno, you did forget to clean up
your toys yesterday. And it's sooo
expensive." The standard pack of five is at
most twenty-five cents. "I don't know if
I have enough money in the budget this month."
He would take out his checkbook and pretend to
tally up figures. "Maybe if we don't buy
groceries next week..." Meanwhile
I'm praying like a maniac and my fingers are
crossed, which results in something that looks
vaguely like a gang symbol. Something I
wouldn't encounter for years. "Well, I suppose
we can make an exception today." He would
reach out and pick the gum adding it to all
the groceries sliding along that black magic
carpet.
Victory.

I am dead though. This gum though, it was so
magical. All those flavors in a strip so
small. And it would always become flavorless
too soon. My taste-buds and jaws are working
like crazy just trying to get out that last
bit of flavor. Sometimes I would even take
the gum out and pull it in all directions,
pressing my tongue against it in hopes that
there would be some flavor hiding somewhere.
It's such a sad thing.
      (Josiah comes close to the
audience, very
      close.)
Flavorless gum. Maybe one of the saddest
things.

*(Looks everyone in the eyes,
shakes his head, takes off his
jacket.)*

When I was *alive* I chewed gum after smoking.
To get it off my breath. I smoked my first
cigarette drunk at a party. A beautiful girl
was smoking, and I felt by taking the
cigarette held in her outstretched hand, the
white tube oh so delicately balanced in her
lithe hand. I thought we would have a
communion of some sort. This Parliament, her
parliament, us smoking out the window.
Tendrils of our plunder rising in the air. We
were entwined by smoke. Like kissing, without
actually touching lips. Her cigarette was
pressed between my lips, and we talked. We
just talked. Never kissed. She never touched
me. She just gave me a cigarette. I know they
kill you eventually,

I was always buying two packs every other
grocery store trip. Cigarettes and Gum. I was
under no delusion about quitting, I had no
desire to do so.

I would smoke as long as it pleased me. Then
one day it stopped pleasing me. And I stopped
buying gum.

Gum. It seems like such a very American
thing. I don't have time to brush my teeth, a
luxury, so I chew on this mass of chemicals
that freshens my breath and whitens my teeth.
So I can go to a fast food restaurant, buy
more food than many people see in a week, eat
it, and chew more gum.

I started smoking after I hugged my grandma
for the last time. She was so skinny, she had
been so big, she seemed inflated almost. Like
an air balloon shaped exactly like a
grandma she would inflate and deflate. When
she walked towards me to say goodbye on the
porch my grandfather built near her trailer,
she crossed each board like they were oceans.
Her breathing ragged, her hands trembling, she
reached out to me. She held me like I was
new, she was so old, and too young to look the
way she did. So old, she held me like I had
just arrived on this earth. She kissed me on
the cheek.
"I love you Josiah."
"I love you too Grandma."
It was the last time I would see my
grandmother. I knew that then. I picked up
those words, and logged them away. I thanked
God they were so easy to remember.

Love should always be the last thing expressed
at a parting.

Better not to part at all.
Better not to die at all.
I might be afraid to die.

I started smoking five years after that.
A girl, someday a grandma.
She gave me my first cigarette.
And we talked.
And I thought about Grandma, spindly, and
trembling on that porch.

She would hate that I started smoking.

It killed her. She would hate it, and I
started, because I
loved that smell, when I held her. Older than
me, but so much smaller than I am. The smell
of cigarettes.
I remember her every time I drag it into my
lungs.

I tell her I'm sorry.

and I smell her memory.

*(another item out of the
pocket)*

A pen. Oh a pen. When I was young I drew all
over myself. Elementary school I would write
notes to myself. I'd outline all my veins. I
would get crushes on the girls who drew things
on me. I used the same pen to write poetry
that I used to outline the contours of my hand
and arms. All that ink, slowly seeping into
my blood. Maybe that's why I have to write.
I'm so full of ink, that it actually is like
breathing, and if I don't breathe out all that
ink I'll die, and if I don't breathe it back
in I can't write.

Anyway.

Ink, all over my body. I loved it, couldn't
stop. I want a tattoo, never got one, but I
had so many when I was
young, peace signs and smiley faces. Big kissy
lips that Sarah drew on me. This is the same
girl that came to school with bright red
lipstick in her backpack. I sat next to her,

and she would raise her hand, get the bathroom
pass. When she came back she had bright
pinky-red lips, and during free time, when we
were all playing slow-motion tag she would run
across the room and smack her lips on the side
of my face, "Ewwww! Gross!" smearing my
pen-stained hand across my face I cried out.
"Ewwww!" My palm would come away from my face
smeared red. Ruby Red Gorgeous. And then from
the other side. "I love you Josiah." And
another big lipstick flooded kiss. Sarah was
smitten, and I thought that girls were just
playmates whom I crushed on from a vast
emotional distance.

Sarah wanted to kiss me on the lips, she told
me so, I wouldn't let her, and she never did.

> *(Josiah pulls another
> object from his pocket.)*

This is my paycheck from my only passion.
Novelist.
I gave a lot of the money away.
I fed myself on minimum wage, so that I could
write my life away. What little money I made,
I donated. I wrote so hard the tips of my
fingers became callused. I feared once that I
might not be a writer, that I might not leave
any kind of legacy. Just once I felt an acute
stabbing pain. What if I'm a shitty writer.

My twenty-something life near its mid-point.
Many monkeys on my back. I'm walking home and
it's
overcast, I'm feeling particularly saddened.
I am struck with the horrifying thought that I

might be a terribly shitty writer. I may in
fact be the world's worst novelist. I walk
past the general store, little stuffed animals
in the window. These little plush toys
intended to cheer little kids only manage to
heighten my panic somehow; a novel about
stuffed animals flashes through my brain. I'm
climbing the stairs next to the Bar-B-Que
place; I can smell the slow cooked meat. My
nostrils flare, and this action sends
acetylcholine to the front of my face, making
my cheeks red, my nose pinkish, and fanning
the flames of my panic. I begin calling
everyone I know, no one answers their phone.
I'm desperate now, I call my mom. No answer.
I call my sister. No answer. My heart is
palpitating and I'm beginning to sweat. As I
reach the pedestrian bridge this writer's
block with knives is digging into my skin.
Ants of doubt are crawling all across my
flesh. I start across this concrete and
chain-link tunnel spanning over the highway.
The clouds shed, and rain drops dart their way
through the canopy of chain link, and I'm
crying. I don't know why I'm crying, but I
am. I'm sobbing, bawling hysterically, and
it's raining, and everything is wet. Not
flooded, or slick, just wet. tepid and wet.
This wet is brushing itself against my
clothing and the walkway. And I'm having this
panic, this insecurity attack. The world seems
to be rotating beneath me, and I wonder why
the hell this bridge seems to last so damn
long. I want to throw myself over the edge. I
want the pavement to rush at me. But this
bridge is encased, with a paint-coated
upside-down half tube of chain-link fence.

I'm trapped, I'm encased, I'm safe. I feel
like I'm stumbling haggard to the end; As I
come to the end of the bridge, I turn, and I
see what God made.
These rolling mountains.
All that green.
Sunlight streaming over the green curve of the
earth like
someone has painted the world with light.
Air thin, but thick with something, air you
can see, oxygen you feel in your lungs.
Doesn't matter if I'm a shitty writer.
Writing is what I do.
It's how I breathe.
I write to stay alive.
That's me.
That's who I am.

I've been told by people who know these things
that my novels are read and studied in
colleges and high schools.
So it goes.

Let's talk about you.
You all are very kind. None of you has left,
that I'm
aware of. Sometimes people sneak out of the
back. But it'd be awfully rude.

This being my death performance and all.
Didn't you know?
This is what I decided to do when I died.
Everyone gets something.
Before that big black curtain, the edge of
never.
I'm just guessing at what it is by the way. I
don't really know. I haven't been there yet.

But you choose, what do you most want to do.
Your deepest desire, and before you face
absolute infinity. You do it.
There's quite a procedure about it. A
well-dressed man in a tailored suit shows up
with papers and brochures, almost like a
travel agency. He lays everything out in
front of you, describes the most popular
options, explains how it's based on merit and
so forth...

"...You see over five-hundred selfless acts
earns you a level five send-off some of the
more popular level fives
include water skiing in the Caribbean, being
the first man to climb Everest, a lovely night
alone with a supermodel of your choosing."

"I'm not really interested in your brochures."

"Really, but we have so many send-offs laid
out here, they
are all very popular."

"What if I want to make one up?"

"Oh well of course we have that, but I must
warn you they're not as controlled as the
standards."

"That's kinda the point, I want to create
one."

"Well then, I suppose that would work."

"I want a theatre, filled with people."

"Okay, yes."

"I want a really, really nice suit."

"Mhmm."

"The one you're wearing is nice, something like that."

"Yes."

"And I want light."

"Yes"

"And that's it."

"That's it, that's all you want?"

"I want the light to be a pull-cord type, like just the bulb, and then standard stage lights."

"Nothing else, no exotic animals? Beautiful co-actors? fancy set?"

"A table. I want a table."

"Right, theatre, suit, lights, table."

"Don't forget the audience."

"Oh I'm sure they're already there."

"Thanks."

"That's all?"

"That's all."

"May I ask you a question?"

"Sure."

"This is the first time I have asked this, of anyone, but... What are you going to do?"

"I'm going to tell them what life is like, and why dying isn't so bad."

"Wait, you mean to say, you want real people out there?"

"Of course. I want living people. If they're just phantoms, dummies, or whatever, what's the point?"

"You want to go back into the real world, with real living people, and be on a stage, and... and what?"

"We'll see."

"You're asking to come back from the dead."

"How else will I explain life from beyond the grave? They have to be alive. If they're fake, if they're a facsimile, they're not fucking real. I need real people. I need to love one more time. I need to tell them the truth of my living and dying experience. I need them. I need them. I need other people, we all do. We all need each other"

(pause)

"You'll have absolutely no control over your
surroundings anything could happen, they might
throw cabbage, or worse. Children might
scream, a man could have a heart-attack. War
could break out. It's the real world, it's not
like death, it's not like the services we
provide. It's life, we can't control that."

"I don't want to die."

"Too late"

"Just put me back in there and enjoy the show.
Record it perhaps, for future patrons."

"It's most unusual, but if you like there's
the door, on your left."

"Thanks."

(Josiah leaves)

"Performing for the living…"

And I walked through the door, and here I am.
Alive again, talking to you about all these
things, these sundry details and so forth.
It's quite a hoot.
(Long pause)
I'd rather not though. I think there's a rule
against that, the dead and the living
copulating.
I'm almost positive there's a rule.
I love this, I love it.

I loved her, and she loved me. You've all had
that, at least once, haven't you? Someone who
moves

against you in the night like drifting sand,
breathes like the ocean, faces so tight
together. I was in love, and I lost her. I
lost her.

We were in love, Casey and I, she was
beautiful, it goes without saying, but she was
stunning, she stunned me. Motionless, she
made me weak and strong, she made me unable
and limitless. She crushed me into an
infinitely small point of light and she made
me feel like a supernova. She was my goddess
and I was her god. We were epic like that.
Time sped up around us because we thought so
quickly together. Days lasted eons. Our days
were filled with the fall and rise of
civilizations. Like this one time, we were
having Chinese food, we were watching a movie,
something animated, and this movie lasted for
all time, each of our movements, when we
bumped knees or when I put my arm around her
shoulder, every movement we made shared our
communication, which was layered, like petals
on a sunflower.

We exchanged thousands of bits of information,
and we had such a constant stream of
communication our minds were strung together.
From across the room, eyes closed, and
mouths shut we could talk. This is the
building block of love, this wordless
sightless communication.

So we're having Chinese food, we're watching
this animated film, and we're moving, not
talking, but we are talking like I told you.
If you've been in a relationship you know this
conversation. Hand to shoulder, knee to
thigh, fingers to back, hair draped over
shoulder. That wordless conversation. Of
course there was this, but we talked too, we
conversed, we moved like a figure skater pair.
And we ate Chinese food. We finished the food,
and milled about the house, cleaning. Picking
up the odd this and that, we wordlessly agreed
that she would brush her teeth and wash her
face first. So she did, and then I did, every
time we passed each other we touched. Casey
would place her hands on my hip to navigate
around me, brush close against me as she
walked into the kitchen. I'd put my hand
against the small of her back directing her
toward the bedroom. Like planets circling
each other, and we'd kiss, only this time we
wouldn't let go. Our bound lips would follow
us into bed, we'd kiss all through taking off
clothes. This is how we spoke, with an eon
long kiss, with clothes removed, with sigh and
breath. Then we'd open our eyes. We'd open
our eyes and we'd be pulled together. I'd
enter her, she'd receive me. Our eyes
together, our bodies together. All of our
conversations were one singular. We'd have
sex, we'd make love, we'd converse, we'd enter
Nirvana together.

And then… We'd move together, with each other.
Our bodies like the waves of the ocean.
Cresting, breaking, a wave again. The shore,
friction against our waves. Our eyes. The

heat of the sun, and then we're moving like,
the rain against the mountains, wind brushing
against peaks. She's pulling me in,
tightening around me. Casey and I, we're
moving like hurricanes, and tornadoes, we're
moving like awakening dormant volcanoes.
We're moving like the earth spinning, circling
in orbit, like the sun moving in rotation
around, a bright hot point of white light, and
we're flooding into that light, our bodies are
liquid, fluid and bursting and our movement
changes the orbit of everything. Our minds
converse, keening, wordless. When we come
back, we dimly become aware of our bodies, and
we feel ourselves. We feel what we are. This
human form. We become familiar with ourselves
again, I'm still inside her, she's still
pulling me, our bodies continue their need. We
left, we're back.

and our hearts are beating. Our heart beats.
We breathe. We'd forgotten. We know our
bodies again, our shoulders, our nipples, our
stomach's our backs, our feet. We lay face to
face, entwined, encircling ourselves, in love.
And we sleep. We sleep the way people forget
how to sleep. The memory you use to have of
sleeping. You slept this way when you were
young. You remembered this sleeping, this is
the way you need to sleep. When you forget
that you're human, you need this sleep, the
post-nirvana sleep, the post-orgasm sleep, the
sleep with another pressed up against you. Our
dreams circle together like smoke-clouds. We
wake up, open our eyes face to face.

Our eyes connected at dawn. We make breakfast like a head and sous chef. All of our movements interchanging and contributing. My hands flipping pancakes onto her plate she holds as she pours more batter. She hands me the orange juice as I set down a glass. Casey and I made breakfast like we spoke, wordless, fluid. And the sound of bacon cooking.
And pancakes sizzling solid.
And eggs cracking.
And our minds spinning together like the tea-cup ride. We eat, and then we converse. If you're outside the conversation we're talking so quickly you can't follow. But to us, our mile-a-minute sentences make perfect sense skipping portions we jointly know, like words, nouns, verbs, phrases, paragraphs. Sometimes we just give each other that look. This is why we don't need words when in each-others presence, but Casey asks me to speak all that time. She loves the sound of my voice. I love the way her lips move. So we talk for pleasure. Because we love how those vibrations feel on our skin. The sounds we make against our bodies. And we leave the house, have cute arguments over locking the door, and turning off the stove. We walk to our Metro stops, and life slams back into normal speed, hours contain the normal amount of minutes, seconds shrink to normal size. We still speak, our bodies exchange electric information, our neurotransmitters all mixed together. We know when to send an encouraging Email, or text something funny about koalas. We operate in unison when separate. We lead our separate professional lives, and Casey

gets home before me. I bring home sushi, because it's sushi night.

She's waiting with a bottle of Cabernet Sauvignon, my favorite. And our day starts again, our night together, our *nights* together, like re-charging, like re-living, baptized daily by love. I lost her though. I died. She's been gone. It's an eternity, not one of our sweet eons. She's been gone. Do you want to know how I died? I bet you do. It's not important. What's more important is how I lived, kindness, compassion, generosity, benevolence, love, desire, all that shit. Did I live a worthy life? Am I performing a worthy death? Did I earn my wings?

Doesn't it just mean enough to want to live in a world like this, to howl into that fucking howl! That's true, an attempt, an attempt and failure at reaching death! That's true! And this thing about Nirvana, the kaleidoscope, the endless field of yellow buzzing energy. That's true. Let me tell you, the reward for living, the reward for not calling it quits is infinite peace, power and pervasive joy. You become everything.

I died. Once. I don't know how it happened. I was on the sidewalk, and then I wasn't. Sorry, I wish I knew more, but I know what happened next.

I'm in the space between sleep and awake, that space where it all blurs together. Then suddenly, I'm stuck in that space. I'm there and I start to lift up; I levitate out of my

body, and as I'm rising out of my body, as my
soul separates from the physical. I become
aware of how very much alive I am, how much
this isn't death, and the moment I think. I'm
Alive! Dammit, Yes! I'm Alive!

As soon as that happens, I'm sucked into a
vacuum of space. I'm catapulted through a
tunnel, an upward tunnel that looks everything
like a kaleidoscope. Only, I'm not looking
through a window into a mess of color and
light. I'm looking right through that edge of
never. It's no black curtain, it's this orgy
of color and light, and this sound, this sound
that's just getting louder and louder, bigger
and bigger, until it's a shattering vibration
running through my bones. It's pulling me
apart, and I'm screaming trying to make it
stop, only my scream doesn't come out. And
suddenly I am this vibration, this screaming.
It's the voice of God, I know it's the voice
of God and it will kill me

The vibrating colors that are me are rushing
toward the end of this tunnel, where there's
nothing but bright white light, I rush so fast
that I'm pulled out into an endless expanse of
white vibrating energy. Just endless light on
light, yellow charged hues. I feel like
infinity and nothingness, an infinitely small
point and an endless expanse at the same time.
I want to live. And when I know that I rush
back out of the light, through the
kaleidoscope tunnel, through the lack of body,
and my soul. My soul slams into my body, and
I'm awake and staring at the ceiling, and I

can't move or breathe. I fear I must have
died.

I've experienced that edge of never.
Certainly that's what happens when we die.
Certainly that's it! Becoming and knowing
everything, and feeling such peace with it
such energy. Breathing everything into your
lungs and exhaling just the same, exhaling
that vibrating soft white, yellow glow.
Forever being a part of the peace which
surpasses all understanding. Diving into it,
becoming it. That's the reward for living
this brutal life.
God finds you.

It felt so good, and I experienced it before
death. Here I am dead finally, and I've
experienced death so many times while I was
alive.
Nirvana.
And that love for Casey.
That's true.
That.
That will always be true.
And the walk across the bridge.
And the cigarettes and the gum.
And the notes.
And the lipstick against my cheek.
And I guess, I guess after all it's so true.
So much of it is true. Hell maybe all of it
is. Maybe everything I say is true.
Truth.
All of it.
All this honey poured all over you!
Honey!
And Kaleidoscopes.

and Gum.

I love you.
I've missed you.
Let's make love.
I love every single one of you.
Do me a favor.
follow me.

You're all still alive.
Just.
Just.
Follow me.

> *(Charges down the center aisle and out the back of the theater.)*

End of Play

[Insert Title of Play Here]

It is of the utmost importance that you produce [Insert Title of Play Here]. It is so important that you produce [Insert Title of Play Here] that I am not going to tell you anything about the play itself, simply why it is important to me that you put [Insert Title of Play Here] on your stage.

I am going to die.

I am going to die soon from starvation.

Unless... Unless, some kind and caring soul produces [Insert Title of Play Here].

Without the potential revenue from this play, I will be unable to pay for food.

—Ah, but there are food stamps.

That's a very good point dear reader. I however have fallen neatly into a category that can neither benefit from food stamps, nor take advantage of other social services.

—What category is that?

I am a college student, and I am still a dependent. I am ineligible for state assistance. My parents still claim me on their taxes, but they have taken away all forms of support both monetary and culinary.

—That's illegal.

True, it is true, dear reader that filing your taxes in such a way is against the law, still somehow my parents seem to have managed it.

—Get a job.

Don't be racist!

—What!? You're white, and what does race have to do with getting a job?

Don't be racist!!

—Listen, if you're going to be illogical, and insulting, I'm certainly not going to produce your play.

Well maybe I don't want my play produced by a racist, it deals very delicately with issues of...

—*Silence.*

...Dear reader, it's clear that these proofs are not enough for you to stage [Insert Title of Play Here]. Please allow me to posit another scenario.

It is of the utmost importance that you produce [Insert Title of Play Here]. It is so important that you produce [Insert Title of Play Here] that I am not going to tell you anything about the play itself, simply why it is important to the **FATE OF THE WORLD** that you put [Insert Title of Play Here] on your stage...

—I've already stopped reading.

Damn.

I'm Building

I'll tell you something. What I'm building...

It's an audacious thing that I'm building in
    here, it has wings and things, and a long
    line of sad whispers you won't ever hear.
    The length of it all is something to
    behold.

I've given it a name, but it's not taking.
    This thing has a mind to break me.

What I'm building doesn't begin or end
    anywhere; it doesn't have a place in this
    world.
                (Turns in his seat)
I'm bringing out the stops, the corked ones
    and marbled glass. I'm drinkin' whiskey
    mixed with grenadine and some sour
    grapes. I have to prepare myself for that
    thing I've been building, because It's
    eyes will take me down.

There's scratches at the door, but the
    formaldehyde has gotten to my head, and
    the horse-like mane that I've been trying
    to cut off of it, has started to turn.

I'd give you a better idea of when to run, but
    I don't rightly know myself, and all I

can say to you is Tom had it right. What
I'm building isn't made for kids. I can
tell you one thing about what I'm
building in here; I can tell you one
thing.

Believe It

(An old man in a hospital gown approaches a child that is waiting at his hospital room door, and grabs his face, sinking his yellowing nails slightly into the child's face.)

Hell has enough logos to put on my chest. I've given all that I have. You'll take some of it out of me in the end, with that hypodermic needle. Sampling me. Biopsy.

You won't know this yet, because you're young.

I'll tell you what you have to look forward to.

(Old man jumps excitedly about.)

There is a box under your bed. A Joe DiMaggio baseball card, a piece of unchewed-opened bubble gum, two marbles, one with a purple swirl and another with a yellow swirl, a free pog cut out of a cereal box.

(Jumping stops.)

You will be seeing me earlier than you
think. In a psychiatric ward in Columbia
Missouri. I'll be in the bed across from
you, with a superman shirt laid out over
my chair, because I don't have any
clothes to call my own.

Run along now, enjoy yourself, you won't
see me for years, and you may never
become me. Climb that tree you always
wanted to climb.

Ode To Beverly

An open letter to Beverly, my 90 year old
landlord who saw fit to criticize my style of
living in a letter thrown on the floor a mere
three days after I signed a lease for my
apartment.

Dear Beverly,

I received your letter yesterday, I understand
you are upset I have no bed. You don't like my
lack of trash cans. And you fear that the
placement of my alarm clock might cause a
fire. Allow me to address these concerns in
this letter, I promise my words will assure
you.

Your concern that I do not have a bed is
touching. As I have just moved in, forgive me
some time to acquire appropriate sleep based
furniture. I have previously lived in
pre-furnished apartments, and as your
dwellings are not such places, I as yet, do
not own a bed, and am perfectly comfortable in
my sleeping bag, which is capable of
withstanding the -85 degree weather of an
Antarctic Peninsula.

I understand that you have concerns regarding
my lack of a trash can in either the bedroom

or the kitchen. Rest assured that trash bags that I have been using to collect my minimal material waste are at present sufficient, as I dispose of them nightly. I did have to buy an additional box of trash bags to handle the trash that manifested itself on my floor between the time you showed me the apartment and the day that I received the keys.

You have mentioned the placement of my alarm clock near the bathroom. It is a sony-dream machine circa 2009 and as such is in accordance with fire regulations and United States consumer code 379B addendum F(C) and will not create an electrical hazard or possible fire by being 8 feet away from shower, sink and toilet. If I were to move it, it would be closer to the kitchen, sink, stove, and oven, therefore twice more likely to cause a fire or other incendiary disturbance.

The final words of your letter, quoted here, "You cannot live like this well." or possibly "You cannot live like this here." Are irrelevant, no matter what version of that sentence your difficult to read handwriting may have penned. I do indeed live well, attending the theater, indulging in spirituous liquors, and frolicking at times that I see fit.

Regarding the second possible version of your statement, I must again draw attention to the fact that I moved in a scant three days previous to your visit. Much of my time thus far is spent sleeping elsewhere, and as I have paid rent and deposit, have not set the residence on fire, do not sell drugs from my kitchen or elsewhere, and am not a prostitute, nor do I engage in any myriad illegal activities, I must politely posit that I take issue with your hard to read judgement of my style of living.

I cannot however reveal, nor do I have knowledge of the possibility of me being a secret agent for a non-governmental organization.

If a slew of black cars arrive at the residence, and suited men and women armed with assorted weaponry dismount and climb their way to my upstairs studio suite, I will have vacated via a helicopter rope ladder, like you see in the movie films.

In that event I will not be paying the next month's rent, and you may keep the deposit.

Sincerely,

—Josh

President of the Universe

Tea Partiers, Anarchists and Flaming Liberal protesters are fond of screaming loudly about how messed up the government is, but very few of them are actively involved in the machinations of bureaucracy.

That is why I, as a Flaming Liberal Anarchist Tea Partier, have decided to run for President of the Universe.

Trust me when I say that I'm not your typical candidate for President of the Universe. Unlike my opponents I have only one head, I am not a hyper-intelligent shade of the color blue, but believe me, within the confines of my one cranium I have enough intelligence to solve all the problems of the universe.

Of course war would be abolished, hunger would be solved with my grandmother's gazpacho, awkward conversations about whether or not someone is available would be eliminated through telepathy.

The real pressing issues facing the humans of the Universe would of course be their inferiority to most interstellar traveling races. I'd assure that we wouldn't be put into camps, or sold into slavery, because humanity has the most fantastic export of all.

Twinkies. It seems that these little blobs of
bread and frosting flavored un-bread and
un-frosting can survive not only nuclear
holocausts and implosions of planets, but also
supernovas and big bangs.

Alien races crave Twinkies not for
consumption, but to reverse engineer for its
use as a shielding for their space-ships.
Financially, the human race would be set.

Running for the president of the universe
isn't easy, believe me, I've been exposed to
more gamma rays than radioactive gerbils, I've
seen things that would turn most people into
little puddles of goo, I once saw blue whales
eaten like sardines on a slice of cosmic
pizza, but I'm more than willing to suffer
through these hardships to become president of
the Universe.

I'm not running for my own glory and benefit,
though infinite youth, beauty, wealth and
health are the standard stipend for the
position. No, I'm running to change the
worlds. I'm running for this position, because
I don't want homeless, nomadic, impoverished,
oppressed, silenced, dumb, deaf, disabled,
psychotic members of the human race to face
another cold night.

I imagine a universe in which babies have a
say about being born, because let's face it,
some of us didn't want to come into this mess
of an existence.

But I envision a universe in which every fetus
will say YES to life. When I become president
of the universe every day will be
ChrismaKwannzaKuhRammalammadingdong day. Joy
will be so prevalent and contagious your
racist grandfather will hug a black dude.
Excitement about living will result in the
spontaneous outbreak of full-length musicals
in social security offices.

Weapons will disappear, instantly, because
when you're President of the Universe, you can
do that kinda thing. Life will be in effect
perfect, unless you choose otherwise because
free will is just too damn awesome.

Change, not just for four years, but for
infinity.

These Things Are Unnecessary

An unnecessary addition to chocolate milk is Ovaltine.

An unnecessary addition to a library is a Dan Brown novel.

An unnecessary addition to a pack of cigarettes is a health warning label about the risks of cancer, I know smoking gives me cancer, which is why I stopped smoking, then I found out that everything gives you cancer, even, possibly, cats. So I started smoking again.

An unnecessary addition to a kitchen junk drawer is organization.

An unnecessary addition to a pop song is a keytar bridge...

No wait, an absolutely necessary addition to every pop song is a keytar bridge.

An unnecessary addition to an awkward first date, is talking about how you will soon be finding a more stable living situation, and you only have a 6-month rent because you need a cheap place to stay while you file for bankruptcy because of your mounting medical

debt due to your psychiatric disorder and your
subsequent multiple stays at the psych ward,
so can it be your place not mine.

An unnecessary addition to that awkward first
date is a second call.

An unnecessary addition to a beach is a
swimming pool.

An unnecessary addition to the moon is an
American flag, due to United Nations ordinance
the moon is owned by no world-government and
is a shared territory administered by the U.N.
and therefore belongs to the people of the
world.

An almost always unnecessary addition to a
joke-off is a Chuck Norris joke.

An unnecessary addition to Chuck Norris is
another fist, but unfortunately for you the
nature of quantum physics dictates that he has
an infinite number of fists to punch your face
an infinite number of times.

An unnecessary addition to a monologue is a
second character.

An unnecessary addition to a series of three
or more is the Oxford Comma, but I like to add
it anyway because I'm a Mother Fucking Rebel.

An unnecessary addition to using the bathroom is an audience, please dear roommate, close the door.

An unnecessary addition to a conversation about existentialism is saying, "Well I feel like existence is intangible. If it does exist, it's probably just a trick of our minds to appease our desire for connection, and something substantial. It's why people get on stage to feel something and feel like a group of people are feeling something with them, but in all honesty we're truly isolated. We can never feel anything, we are alone." To which I always respond. "That's cool, I'm gonna go to my weekly Fight Club."

An unnecessary addition to me making a cliche joke about Fight Club is someone saying, "The first rule of Fight Club is, don't talk about fight club."

How To Reverse Time

Rustle through broken leaves; pull them
together like puzzle pieces.

Speckle shattered branches with pages of
green; bind fragmented arms together with
vines. Lift new-formed

limbs against the shedding bark. Dip your
fingers in honey; smooth the branches with
your palms. Stack segments of trunk, ordering
them according to their rings. Build this

oak from its riven, and water it with your
tears. Dry your eyes, and sit under the shade
of the life you restored;

dream of lost souls re-making their trees
while you slumber.

Chicago Public Schools For a Day

(In imaginary straight jacket)
Last year this school went through 15 other
teachers in this classroom. Three of the
students came directly from psychiatric
institutions.

The day before I was supposed to teach the
class there was a substitute. I was observing
the students, and assisting with routines and
procedures, rules and steps for entering the
halls and lining up for lunch and so on...

I thought I could do this.

I was wrong.
(Struggling to get out of straight jacket)
Returning from a meeting with the principal, I
saw Student T. throw his chair into his desk
and against the wall. Students D and K ran
around the room punching and kicking each
other and other students. Student J was
mutilating himself with a pencil, he had scars
up and down his leg. And he was smiling and
laughing quietly. Student W said, "Are you
scared."

These kids are 8 to 11 years old.

My blood was concrete. I could hear myself

screaming inside my mind, so loudly that my
heart sounded tinny and nonexistent.
       (Giving up on straight jacket)
I'm sorry I'm not strong enough for you.

I like to tell myself that someone will be
someday,

I know that might not happen.

I'm sorry.

The World as a Rose

The human hand cannot hold
the red & white petals from
growing out of thorns.

The stems have no hold
of their thorns. Do not destroy
a rose, we must protect our decisions

with the rights of a flower.
The Earth has granted a rosebush
the ability to be alive, the opportunity

to grow, the fortitude to withstand
time, space & color blindness.
A rose cannot be stolen

from its berth just as a boat
will flounder when, commandeered.
Roses are bereft of care.

They do not give a fuck about you,
me or anyone else. The thorns,
seldom known fact, are slightly

poisonous. Do not mess with a rose.
Do not mess with a thorn,
unless you desire a silk & seductive

death. It is customary to give a white
rose in time of immense mourning,

funerals, national tragedies. We are

gifted with life from a miraculous
unfolding lotus; don't allow the rose
to poison you, because she is here

to redirect our idiocy. The world
allows us to live upon it. It cannot be owned.

Outbound

Flight is calling me, I'm giving up gravity
for once. Take out those steam pressed slacks
and your terry cloth tie, because we've been
given lease to let out into the world, and try
something new for a change.

I'd like to tell you right now that we don't
have a lot of change in our pockets. None to
give and little to buy a drink with. We'll run
barefoot across tacks if we have to. Because
our destination is just too damn important not
to gain ground.

Let's play king of the hill and bobby of the
valley. I'd like to lay low under bridges that
are collapsing so I can feel the weight of
failure. But that bridge carried so many
across into a place that I can't even begin to
reach, because I'm stuck here under all this
rubble.

Give me a hand and lift me up. Holding onto
the pieces of each other that keep us happy,
like helping me out of a pile of junk. I'll
bring an apple I found, we're gonna need it.

Roll that apple down into the vale, rip open
the seeds and let's grow trees. Let's build a
bubble around this tree and call it Earth.
We're happy enough to bring the galaxy here.

We're home and now we can act like it. A tree for every planet and enough apples to go around, thank God.

Weave A Little Sinew, Drink A Little Whiskey

Looms run forever, threading fate faster than
your hand rallies against an avalanche of
stones. If you are without sin, step forward;
cast flowers; shower the underclass, land

paupers. When they till the soil, moving more
than sand, exhalations of thanks vibrate the
air. Clasp fate you'll win looms. Run forever,
threading fate. Faster than your hand,

your eye captures moments. Be careful, don't
linger or stand in one second too long, lest
you miss the song of merry men step forward.
Cast flowers, shower the underclass' land;

prosperity runs deep through all dreams both
planned and spontaneous. Even royalty must
understand their kin; looms run forever.
Threading fate faster than your hand

determined beggars toil against sleet and tan.
Understand, never has the merchant, till kings
embrace them as kin *step forward; Cast
flowers, shower the underclass' land*

water and loam. Watch as the crops grow
unmanned. Every extension of the body pulses
and will begin looms. Run forever, threading
fate faster than your hand; step forward, cast

flowers; shower the under-class-land.

Sunrise

My throat full, I began to realize
a pain from my arm with the IV,
and for the first time, I saw the sunrise.

Walking to the hospital window, I rise
on my tiptoes stretching completely.
My throat is full. I began to realize

my hands are the perfect size
to lift this window pane easily,
and for the first time, I saw the sunrise.

Cars below as midwest time flies.
I'm crying now, coughing discreetly,
my throat full; I began to realize

that my feet carry me, please
give me grace, kiss me sweetly,
and for the first time. I saw the sunrise

across the horizon, reach across lies
beyond the window, the lock frees.
My throat full I began to realize,
and for the first time, I saw the sunrise

Funny, How Some Walk Into The Smallest Spaces

Thinks the man strolling towards me, bicuspids
solidly thrashing themselves against lettuce
stuck between his teeth. Tim—I have decided
to call him— rages at this lettuce,
eviscerating it and pulling trailing
xylem and phloem out of its green plain into
the back of his mouth.

Newspaper nutritional value stamped solidly in
its dynamic ribose nucleotides; the sticker
reads that one serving should take longer to
eat than water, but hopefully have the same
effect: calories from fat are zero, grams of
fat are zero, grams of green, half. Marijuana
this is not, which leads me to wonder what
purpose

lettuce serves as it washes past the uvula.
Where in the grand scheme of life are we
going to need green solid water? Soon
environmental destruction will take our
lettuce from us; I wish now, eating this page,
that my newspaper nutritional value was a
little tastier. Tim with the stomach-acid
eating

through his meal *for* him had it right. Queer
that he would be squeezing limbs into the
space between me and a wall with a head of
iceberg. That Martian I just pressed between
my molars kissed my teeth, as the Sirens of
Titan quieted heavenly wails. I pause,
because the reason Tim with the lettuce

squidged himself soundly against my pulsating
veins, (xylem and phloem) occurred to me.
Eventually we all go to Titan; proximity
expands our ability to breathe life into our
lungs. Dream Titan looks as follows, no
lettuce, no bicuspids owned by Tim; only
books, forks, and incisors feeding titanic
earthlings.

Genetic Engineering From the Egyptians to the CIA

Egyptian gods hold my mother's name above
their heads in hieroglyphics. They travel up
the Nile, paper-thin, and painted. My friend
Seth has a similar painting hanging in the
corner of his living room; sometimes I pretend
that
all these pseudo Egyptians are in a coalition,
dishing out sacrificed and charred

meat at their conferences, tracking persons of
interest like some ancient, overly,
established CIA. Then I wrench out of my
reverie. They are paintings probably purchased
at a craft fair. Definitely not an ancient
artifact, or certificate of a secret society,
definitely not. Life's simple convolutions
rarely include

the supernatural or mystique laden intrigues
of ancient societies. The meat at the
conference is drying up, its succulence
fading. Water evaporates off the skin of the
meat; dry steam mixes with dry words. It's not
a ritual sacrifice, it's a barbeque, ritual
but not sacrificial. I cut the ribs with a
spoon, allow

the beef to dissolve in my mouth. This
Barbeque is the consistency of meat clouds. A
man walks up to me, he is wearing a black
suit, black tie, black aviators, and Fedora.
Raising a spoon full of meat between us, he
winks back at my smile. He then takes off his
glasses, placing them between us. I smile

again, he winks.

He slides a document across the greasy table;
I pick up the greasy manila envelope. He
smiles, I wink. He walks away, and dissipates
three feet from the edge of our families white
picket fence. I pull out a lighter crack it
open, and pour its watery contents over the
envelope painting it flammable. It burns up
like my altered genetic history, and collapses
like former empires. The pyramids are burning
releasing hieroglyphic smoke signals sent to
Seth, my mother, and the invisible suit.

Still Riding the Bus

Public transportation renders Taylor's mind
and body docile; sleeping on cushions
stiffened with age, head pressed against the
seam between steel and window pane, because
that is where the head naturally nestles, but
the resulting thwack when the bus bumps
eventually becomes too much: the punch of
rigid metal against the temple, she has
started wearing well padded hats purchased for
a dollar from the Eagle Cares thrift store, to
circumvent the collision, and she sleeps to
lose a race against the deprivation rift
created by the sixty four hour toil, two jobs
is like an ant carrying a dead ant, yet this
bus will tire too, gears and pistons refusing
to gear or piste, marrow refusing to flood the
arteries with cells, engine coils snapping
uncoiled, neurons without enough electricity
to fire mite tiny neurotransmitters between
synapses (that gap left vacant like a parking
lot at a MLS practice), and Taylor decays more
quickly, not owning a car, she rails against
those minutes, hours, years, lost by the
commute; somehow she grows fatter, somehow she
grows older, somehow her bucket list shortened
to accommodate the holes growing in her shoes:
stolen loaves of bread from King Soopers make
terrible patches—stolen hearts don't make gaps
gapless—and though her beauty will wane, her
unfinished college degree from Mesa state will

remain, complete days lusterless never
regained, she thanks the impact of her head
against the window pane; it reminds her to
ever search as she straggles, off-kilter,
drunken, and halfway across the street
jugglers path of mistakenly flung flaming
torches, passably sane: her shifty eyes only
align when she's had her fill of dandelions,
her aching muscle tissue only relaxes to the
sound of butterflies sucking nectar, magnified
when the anarchist puts aside his megaphone
without turning it down, her scrambling mind
only calmed by adding salsa, and losing the
Cascade for the dishwasher lengthens her
chores irreversibly—Taylor cuts these carrots,
a Christmas present from her mother, until
they are shavings and places them atop her
television before the syndicated rerun of MASH
distracts her from reading Organic Chemistry:
Level Three, and though she is allergic, the
bumble bee outside will never encounter her
flesh.

The Most Important Person in the World

What if you were already famous?
You didn't know your own story,
the truth that defines you.

People throw parties at their
home for your victories, crying
when you have the worst day of

your life. Tragedies put whole
companies out of work for weeks.
This is your *Truman Show* life.

An hour means 2.7 million in ad
sales. Your life will be syndicated
and shown on TLC until

the end of all things. When you
finally graduated from college
there was a riot of celebration

in Frankfurt, Germany. It's true
you are the most important
person in the world. Congratulations.

Even your family loves you...
especially your family, because
you are special and worthy.

Villanelle

Refrain one, stop.
Line two, roll;
Refrain two, drop—

—line four, top.
Line five, stroll...
Refrain one, stop.

Line seven, crop
line eight, pol.
Refrain two, drop—

—line ten, chop
line eleven/toll.
Refrain one, stop

line thirteen. Pop
line fourteen! Null
refrain two, drop

line sixteen, slop:
line seventeen. Goal:
refrain one, stop.
Refrain two, drop—

The Power Company

The power company has knitted it's brow;
Our house is plunged into darkness.
What solutions to life will we Google now?

We'll light candles and share stories about
how we love each other, and we will fight
through this. The power company has knitted
it's brow,

and we have no way to cook, so we'll plow
onward and read Junot Diaz. What solutions to
life will we Google now

that light is no more? Thee and thou
we'll find by firelight in Shakespeare's
treatise. The power company has knitted it's
brow,

but we've closed our fists, and started a row,
and we've got literature by the fingerful
webless What solutions to life! Will we Google
now?

Not a damn thing, there's no need we endow
ourselves with the written and spoken
screenless. The power company has knitted its
brow; what solutions to life will we Google
now?

Improvised

There was a recent study about improvisation
stating that the practice of the art enhances
plasticity of the brain and facility of
creation.

A TEDx presenter gave a compelling
demonstration
that showed neuron firing increases.
There was a recent study about improvisation

called a scene, on a stage, a presentation
of the facility of the art that pleases
plasticity of the brain. And, facility of
creation

can be achieved by line recitation,
but no lines allows unlimited places
there. Was a recent study about improvisation

a child exploring infinity through
imagination?
I believe that's the way humanity traces
plasticity of the brain and facility of
creation.

Given time to imagine without cessation
whether there be none or a million faces.
There was a recent study about improvisation,
plasticity of the brain and facility of
creation.

The Recession

The Great Recession waits for the train,
and it has a few dimes in it's pocket;
it will ride across the midwest plain.

Great minds have been driven insane,
desperately clasping a sweetheart locket.
The Great Recession waits for the train,

but it may not arrive. Explain
to the world plugged into a socket,
it will ride. Across the midwest plain

children need their meds to maintain
a sense of sanity, minds as the Challenger
rocket;
the Great Recession waits. For the train

will not roll or speed, and mothers complain
about living without a plot. Sit,
it will ride across. The Midwest plain

lays awake, a woman in the rain
with no money she can't give a shit.
The Great recession waits for the train;
it will ride across the Midwest, plain.

The Reach of Wall Street

New York, you don't know my name.
Your avenues are unfamiliar to me, yet
I feel the reach of Wall Street.

Your stone has smashed my face in
consistent with your promises.
New York, you don't know my name

or where I live, but I know your
son. He's been out late and didn't call.
I feel the reach of Wall Street.

He's grabbing at my vulva,
Blue Label on his breath,
New York, you don't know. My name

is a secret, nameless I'll press on.
Someday I will spend where I cannot
feel the reach of Wall Street

stumbling for the light,
but grabbing at my health instead.
New York, you don't know my name;
I feel the reach of Wall Street.

America is Dead After Allen Ginsberg

Mr. Ginsberg your America was bitter and
tasteless;
I hated it, and I was taught to become hate in
the form of burning red orchids. I saw all
that America was and there were knives, but
futures
were not so cut and sour, despoiling in
Wastelands so well described by T.S. Eliot
There was hope and anti-everything that was
stripping us of your dignity.

Radicalism was born within the world as a bird
flying from the corrupt shell of its sphere.
Ginsberg I am sorry to say that your attempt
to save America was a waste, a shadow of
pestilence, wrought from the stupidity of
those who had control, and combated by too
few.

I weep to tell you that those great few are
gone. They have died and the impotent
Radicals are ostracized.
Even those who are taught to give voice
silence those with vicious mutterings
Human connection has been circumvented
by human indifference.
The problem is global. Your America is dead,
and we killed it by walking
away while it lay with the prong of a nuke in
its neck. It was probably the one that the
nun spilled her blood on.

My mother loves America and
will come to your door without a warrant and
smash you over the head.

My mother will water-board you until death, or
beat your organs till they fail.
But it's okay as long as King _____ the Second
deems it so.

Psych wards make the sane crazy, repetition
battering at their minds. They can't
prescribe properly anyway. New prejudices are
arising, when it is no longer proper
to discriminate based on what you can see, we
must discriminate based on invisible urges
others have to deal with our own impulse to
deviance. We pretend to celebrate diversity,
isn't deviance diversity?

America and my mother agree that we should
place identification cards with tracking chips
in the wallets of every single United States
citizen. America wants to put little push
pins on a map and in every immigrant to the U.
S. and A, so that they can keep track of their
progress in achieving the American Dream with
every single tiny world intelligence agency
broadcasting every step they take. Even my
Mother is a bit scared by this.

My mother claims marriages must not be equal
because the Bible considers it a sin. Many
Christians say that all sin is wrong.
Christians say that being Gay is a wrong.
That means if you are Gay you have committed
all sins. But Christians are born with sin.
That means Christians are wrong...So that means
that every single Christian is gay, and why
shouldn't they be. We lost joy when the
burning Bush arrived to scorch white oval
offices.

God considers a sin. Wasn't suicide a sin?
Did Christ commit suicide?
Ginsberg, I digress.

Today my mother is America.

When will we approach America with a banana
and demand that we have our rights back, lest
we sodomize it ritualistically?
Is that absurd of me to say? Maybe you should
look at what is happening in our government,
and then re-evaluate what you think the term
absurd means.

I am the essence of Absurdity and it is with
this power that I fight our America.

Ginsberg, what happened to Socialism? It was
an ideal.
Modification could have saved us all, now I am
attacked every day.

Ginsberg are you still there? Do you believe
in an afterlife? Because if you do,
we want you back.

There are no acting radicals left alive,
general malaise and apathy have fallen like
gnats
upon the neurons of my generation. Television
is the opiate that keeps us in line to watch
the hanging; little do we know that it is our
own.

America has died, Mr. Ginsberg. Allen are you
there? Can you hear me?

Allen did you die when America died?

I knew we were fucked anyway.

I wish I could say that God could bless what
you might become, but I fear that God has
turned his back on you America, for fear of
getting hurt again, not to mention your
misrepresentation of his names. I believe he
is considering litigation.
God can't save you America. Let us heal you
if we can.

America I hate you. I truly and sincerely do.
I wish you all the best in your conquest
of other's souls, and hope that you arrive at
the gates of judgement soon.

America you're killing my body.
America you killed my soul.
God bless what you could have been

Do We Still Shine?

Luster has left the world. She came to us and
found the nations wanting.
It is a kindness that she left. The gleam that
remains "when ya did something real good." is
a lie told to us by our grandfather when you
fetch him his cigarettes.

The Marlboro man is here and sooner or later
he will take his due. There is no pool in
Southern California that can save you from the
ash. Fukushima is poisoning the Pacific, but
it doesn't matter. We will all be underwater
soon. "Here's the end; get your gills today"

Luster left with grandfather time, he found
that his work was done as our days.
We have brought ourselves to the brink of
waiting for our breakfast quiche
With a sneer in our mouths while our barista
can barely buy Nissan Ramen.

Where did the moments of quiet chess playing
against ourselves go?
We achieved stalemate high fived our solo
conquest, and then left the board
To the dogs. There is no lookout for our kings
as they are waiting on their squares.

They will be trampled by, ready, aim, hold
your breath to steady the scope, watch

As this bullet sails through nitrogen, oxygen,
helium particles to find it's target.
Our presidents are all dead. We've put puppets
into the home that slaves

Built. And we painted that fucker, white? We
are the white America. We are the wrong
America. My ancestors stole everything from a
nation that already had nations of people. We
take our God and cast every stone we can find.
These stones have been run smooth by a blood
letting. I will not subdue my rage. Once we
"made America great again" my lymphocytes
boiled out of my body.

These white blood cells released from this
coil running electrically wild. Powering over
the JavaScript that held the barrier between
me and that orange fuckers face. I texted my
friend that night, "Do you want to start a
revolution?" He responded with an "ellipses."

Luster has gone from this world. There are no
longer silver dreams for us to hang our bowler
cap on. Godot is not coming. We will go. We
will wait. We will not stop screaming at the
brick wall of our prison. All we needed was a
room with a view; now there is no light coming
through the window. It has been bricked up.

I ask, "Why are you not angry?" And all I get.
Dot. Dot. Dot. Have we been satiated by the

currency tit. Pouring forth that mother's milk. Cramming that mad Max shit down our throat. Cramming that Brown Coat hope down our throats. Cramming that long dark tea time down our throat. Cramming that luster of the silver screen, of the digital pseudo-life, of the flat thick dead trees with stale words down our throat. Cramming the amniotic fluid of our lackluster birth back down our throat. The truth is we were never born. The truth is we are all dead.

We are walking through the near death experience that is living in America. This is my America; this is your America. Haven't you wondered why there is no America?

We have let America pick at our bones and strip us into stew food. We are swirling around the drain at the end of a discarded spoon.

America is the spoon. America is the luster. America has been taken by force, and we are all victims to the mad ship captain intent on driving us into the maw at the end of the ocean. This captain is Ahab. This captain is Nemo. This captain is an astronaut so intent on getting back to the cockpit that he would leave his whole crew in the vacuum of space, watch as their lungs asphyxiated and their suits imploded, their bodies crystallizing and

exploding in space. This captain would watch
and laugh at the comfort of the ship he took
by sheer hate.

What Luster? Are you not mad America? Are you
not mad? "Do you want to start a revolution?"
Ellipses. Ellipses. Ellipses.

America Alive Yet

We are here, America; we are the unmarried
queer America. We are the here & now Eckhart
Tolle, self help book extraordinaire America.
We are about to implode & overload Old
Faithful Yellowstone without Gold America.

We are the queens of America. America, your
almighty dollar will one day fail, america.
You were supposed to represent freedom now you
take away lives; after all your chief export
is weaponry & biological tourism terror
America.

There is nothing left to copyright anew, and
every last Disney movie will make too much
money. Tell Disney the truth, America. You
have too many stories on download & now the
price of art is approaching zero.

America you have this to yourself and the
State of the Union is weak and afraid America.
Why is there another Trayvon Martin, Eric
Garner, Vegas & Texas Church massacre everyday
America? WE don't have a shovel to dig
ourselves out of this Colorado oil pit you are
fracking us into America, you are fraudulent
and pushing everyone else off the life raft
America.

Your heart is barely beating, and your constitution is dying America. We have to 3D print hope in the shape of Teddy bears America. China will only supply us with the most faulty broken phones, and as soon as your iPhone refuses to load it's screen you will have to recalibrate yourself, and be a better example to your people because your phone costs more than $900 it costs children's lives America.

America I love you, but you're bringing me down. America I can't leave you; try unity now. America you've infiltrated yourself, and you've lost against flowers; if only you had a coin to spare we'd give you a red, white, and blue rose. Earn your stripes back & and I'll give you a daisy for your Schoolhouse Rock America.

America I'm tired, please leave me alone. America I'm tired please give me my leave. America I'm done, and I'd like to go home. America please recommend the best street to sleep on and allow me for a night to not be picked up by police. Allow me one night to rest my knees. Allow me one night to plant myself and become a tree...

But even Washington was known for cutting them down. America, if you ever again are required to use Skulls & Bones as a way to fertilize your soil, I recommend you leave the Natives alive, and throw Manifest Destiny in the trash.

America, if you love Christianity so much, consider kneeling and presenting all the Benjamins in your wallet to the next homeless person you see. Christ would not behave like you America, but don't be ashamed, just grow more sunflowers America.

Just grow some compassion America, just grow less money America, grow less monopoly, grow your light America, grow your Impressionist exhibit America, grow your lucid dreams America, grow old america, and grow wise enough to embrace your children, and kind enough to cook them dinner.

I want to grow old enough to share my last peace pipe with you America. I want to outlive you America, because a Parent should never have to bury their child, but if the occasion called for it, I would bury you in the clover with many bees, and let them sting me till I die with you, because at the end of the day.

I love you America, and honey will fuse us together, and maybe heal these open wounds you have given me. Peace, paize, repose, there are lives yet to live America, and as we arrive we will leave you, naked & wanting.

Millennialism

We came searching for handouts and sure
dreams. We arrived before we started classes
and expected all of our books to be paid for
by our parents. We graduated with a long way
to go, before the world would consider us
adults.

We came into this world kicking and screaming,
and we left/were fired from our first office
job the same way. Our generation may know the
end of death, and we chat about it as
nonchalantly as we take our Abilify. We hold
what once was considered a super computer in
our hands in order to ignore the onset of
infinity.

Forever, with its abyss, is swallowing us up
like apples. Forbidden fruit has become Our
breakfast, by which I mean we've destroyed all
social convention and we are all fucking each
other, either sexually or professionally or in
the mind.

We are bereft, we are lossless, we stalk the
streets drinks in hand, cigarettes in mouths,
drugs in every vein if we D.A.R.E. We can't
shock you anymore, because we are all bound
for the electric chair. We might become more
machine than man, before we know the end of

things. The world is buckling under the weight
of our consumption. We have consumption.

Ashley has dysentery. Ashley has died. We
learned that people die by playing The Oregon
Trail; someone in a country we can't

comprehend has died of a disease we only ever
see in green
glowing letters. We are self absorbed. We are
hopeless. We are
useless. We care more than anyone born before
us, we are horrified.

We can do nothing, because so few of us have
anything. We have been abandoned by a world
that told us to follow our dreams. We are
mostly American, and most of us are uneasy
about it. Some of us have left permanently.

We would like to know if you want fries with
that. We want to know where the hell that
layer went in Photoshop. We would like to know
if you are allergic to penicillin. We would
like to know why we have to proofread this
bill, when congress won't read it. We would
like to change the world, but it is doubtful
we will run for president, because fuck that
shit.

We would still like to believe the system will
one day work. We are running as fast as we

can, and we can't see the end. We are tired of
insane people running for office. We are, most
of us, insane. We have, most of us, been to a
therapist. We have yelled about
our parents to a stranger. We are weary and
weak, we have wept and we have forgiven us,
for we know not what we have done.

We have abandoned faith or we have never had
it. We are one with the mystics. We came back
to church to challenge authority. God was dead
before we showed up, so it's not our fault.
Ask the murderers. Ask your neighbor for a cup
of sugar. Do any of us remember that, that was
a thing? We are missing everything necessary
to be whole, yet we are so earnest.

We try hard, and we care about each other, and
we want what's best for everyone, and we are
all going to fail, because we are competing
with each other, and there's only so much
bread, and so much money, and so much water,
and let's privatize that while we're at it.
Great fucking move there.

We are private about nothing; we post publicly
about everything. Our necks are arching, and
our backs were broken a long time ago by
standardized tests. We've taught for America
and found that it didn't make the grade. We
are failing you my dear.

We are already in detention. We will not look up to say hello, either because of our phones, or because we are in a hurry, or because we have every reason to be afraid. We are long past closing time.

We are now old enough to see someone we used to know, living homeless and mad on the red line in Chicago. We are without hope even though we voted for it. We are working so hard, because even if the world ends, at least we won't have done nothing. We have done nothing, we are already gone.

We are here to stay, and we are worth every penny. We will carry this backpack packed for us by everyone else on our back. We will usually ford the river. We are a stone rippling in the oceans of time. Don Bluth raised us, we are personally acquainted with NIMH. Adventure, whimsy and all that bag of shit, on earth as it is in heaven. When this world fades away, we will care more.

We cry a lot, alone and in groups. Why isn't everyone crying?
We pay attention. We were born ready for the earth to explode any minute.

We are the first generation to know that Mother Earth is totally fucked.

We are the only ones complacent in our rage.
We want to share an apple with you, but it's
filled with Chromium-10. WebMD says we died
yesterday.

Why wouldn't we be neurotic? Why wouldn't we
be scared? Why wouldn't we D.A.R.E. to do
every substance under the sun. We are stuffing
every gun with every flower we can find, and
we fight for everyone, because we want what's
best, we deserve what's best, we give our
best.

We will pull the marrow from our cancer bound
bones, and let America chew us alive. We've
given up, we've given everything, we have no
soul to give.

Every generation hates us since they started
naming generations, I guess that makes us
Judas Iscariot, who walks more closely with
Jesus than we do. We've won olympic medals,
we've cured Ebola, we've written the next
great American novel, we've

sold out our Monster's Ball. We've got more
degrees than the Bible's got psalms. We've
seen planes become bombs, and we are ready to
lift the towers back up.

We've left the pity party behind. We want you
on our side. We are, like it or not, the

future. We have our orders, we are marching,
we are trite, we are overdone, we are the
first of our kind. We are going to live
forever; we can see the edge of the world from
here. Will you come with us?

Joshua C. Robinson

Haiku

Leaves are always blown
by the wind that does not cease.
Life always finds us.

ABOUT THE AUTHOR

Joshua Robinson received degrees in Playwriting
and Poetry from the University of Missouri; he
also completed a Master's of Arts Management at
Columbia College Chicago. His work has been
featured or is forthcoming in The Maneater, The
Vail Mountaineer, Newcity, Life and Literature in
Performance, Mizzou New Play Fest, The Edge
Theatre, Hemingway's Playpen and more.

Made in the USA
Monee, IL
10 July 2021